D0516583

Crows and Ravens

NATURE WALK

Crows and Ravens

James V. Bradley

CHELSEA
CLUBHOUSE
An Imprint of Chelsea House Publishers

CROWS AND RAVENS
© 2006 by Infobase Publishing

All rights reserved. No part of this book may be reproduced or utilized in any form or by any means, electronic or mechanical, including photocopying, recording, or by any information storage or retrieval systems, without permission in writing from the publisher. For information contact:

Chelsea Clubhouse
An imprint of Infobase Publishing
132 West 31st Street
New York NY 10001

Library of Congress Cataloging-in-Publication Data

Bradley, James V. (James Vincent), 1931–
  Crows and ravens / James V. Bradley.
     p. cm. — (Nature walk)
  Includes bibliographical references and index.
  ISBN 0-7910-9115-5 (hardcover)
  1. Crows—Juvenile literature. 2. Ravens—Juvenile literature.
  I. Title. II. Series: Bradley, James V. (James Vincent), 1931– Nature walk.
  QL696.P2367B73 2006
  598.8'64—dc22   2006011765

Chelsea House books are available at special discounts when purchased in bulk quantities for businesses, associations, institutions, or sales promotions. Please call our Special Sales Department in New York at (212) 967-8800 or (800) 322-8755.

You can find Chelsea House on the World Wide Web at
http://www.chelseahouse.com

TEXT AND COVER DESIGN by Takeshi Takahashi
ILLUSTRATIONS by William Bradley
SERIES EDITOR Tara Koellhoffer

Printed in the United States of America

BANG PKG 10 9 8 7 6 5 4 3 2 1

This book is printed on acid-free paper.

All links and Web addresses were checked and verified to be correct at the time of publication. Because of the dynamic nature of the Web, some addresses and links may have changed since publication and may no longer be valid.

TABLE OF CONTENTS

Chapter 1

Introduction to Crows and Ravens

History of the Crow

CROWS AND THEIR CLOSE RELATIVES, ravens—the largest members of the crow family—are an important part of the history of civilization, from before ancient Egypt to modern Europe and North America. The Native Americans of the northwestern United States honor the crow in their religious dances. Crows are also seen in carvings on ancient tombs in the Middle East, in modern comic books about Vikings, and in children's fairy tales about wicked witches. Perhaps because of their **scavenger** habits, their black color, and their loud calls, crows often spark negative feelings.

In accounts of the Middle Ages (around A.D. 400–1500), crows were often noted as gathering before a battle, knowing they would be able to get an easy meal with all of the dead bodies that would be left after the fight. It is said that before the Battle of Agincourt between the English and the French began in 1415, crows gathered in the trees on the French side, predicting (accurately, as it turned out) the French defeat. Over the years, observations like these led people to associate crows with death.

In an old Viking folktale, Odin, one of the Viking gods, was an ignorant fellow who wanted to conquer the world. He hired two ravens, named

The crow's black color and loud voice often spark negative reactions among human observers.

Many cultures believe that crows and ravens have links to the world of the dead.

Thought and Memory, to fly around the world and report back to him on what was happening. The two ravens flew off each day and enjoyed themselves. Then they returned each evening and made up reports about various events: wars being fought, treasures found, and beautiful maidens captured. Odin foolishly believed every word and paid the sneaky ravens well.

In many cultures crows are sometimes seen as messengers that bridge the gap between the living and the dead. Nineteenth-century American writer Edgar Allan Poe's poem "The Raven" is a perfect example of this.

But not everything about crows and ravens is negative. We can look at crows with humor. They are often portrayed in folklore, cartoons, and comic movies as characters of intelligence, cleverness, wit, and humor, even if they are being shown as con artists and comic villains.

Crow and Ravens Anatomy

Crows and ravens are very dark, and their color helps them survive. At night, the most dangerous time for most birds, the crows and ravens' color protects them from owls, their most feared predators. Crows and ravens were originally forest birds that fed mainly in trees. Their black color may have kept them safe in the dense, shaded forests. Even today, these birds

AN EXCERPT FROM EDGAR ALLAN POE'S "THE RAVEN"

Open here I flung the shutter, when, with many a flirt and
   flutter,
In there stepped a stately raven of the saintly days of yore;
   Not the least obeisance made he; not a minute stopped
      or stayed he;
   But, with mien of lord or lady, perched above my
      chamber door—
Perched upon a bust of Pallas just above my chamber
door—
      Perched, and sat, and nothing more.

Then this ebony bird beguiling my sad fancy into smiling,
By the grave and stern decorum of the countenance it wore.
"Though thy crest be shorn and shaven, thou," I said, "art
   sure no craven,
Ghastly grim and ancient raven wandering from the Nightly
   shore-
Tell me what thy lordly name is on the Night's Plutonian
   shore!"
      Quoth the Raven, "Nevermore."

prefer to rest and sleep in groves of dense trees. They
are often separated from one another by long distances as they search for food or defend their territory. Their black color makes it easy for them to spot
other crows or ravens at a distance.

Crows' eyes have a whitish **nictitating** membrane that rises in front of the eye. This membrane

The raven has a strong, massive bill that curves at the end.

cleans and protects the eye, keeping it moist. The membrane is also used to communicate with other crows as it opens and closes.

The crow's bill is strong, narrow, and pointed. It is a good tool for defense as well as for feeding. The raven's bill is bigger, and the upper part of the bill curves at the end. By lowering the floor of the mouth and pulling the tongue back, crows and ravens can form a pouch for carrying food.

Although crows and ravens appear to be black, their feathers are iridescent and look deep blue and purple in the sun.

Crows have six pairs of muscles that control their "voice box." This helps explain crows' ability to mimic many different sounds. Songbirds have from seven to nine muscles controlling the voice box, while most other birds have only two or three.

The crow's black feet and legs are covered by scales. They have three toes that extend forward, with one extending backward. This three-one combination is ideal for perching. The crow hops, walks, and runs, often in humorous combinations.

When crows fly, their wings form a V-shape. The wings of a raven (seen here) are horizontal.

The "black" feathers of ravens and crows are actually deep purple and blue with an **iridescent** sheen. This sheen can make crows appear lighter when they fly in bright sunlight. Some Native American tribes believed that this sudden bright flash was a sign of the crow's spirit. The iridescence also makes subtle communication signals like tail flicking easy for crows to see from a distance.

When gliding or soaring, the wings of a crow form a V-shape. A raven's wingspan, on the other hand, is horizontal. Larger in size, the raven weighs about three times as much a crow. Ravens puff out their ear, neck, and belly feathers to look larger when they are threatened or are trying to scare other ravens.

You can't tell the sex of a crow by looking at its external anatomy. Determining sex can be done with a **DNA** analysis from blood or by making a small cut to locate the testes or ovaries. You can also figure out the sex of some crows, like dominant males and nesting females, by watching their behavior.

The muscles in the crow's skin give the bird fine control of its feathers. If a crow is unsure of a situation, it will rapidly spread and close its tail feathers. This lets other crows know that there may be danger. Tail flicking is used in courting and in a variety of ways to express how an individual bird feels. The feathers that cover the crow's head also signal many emotions and moods. The head feathers are especially useful in showing dominance, anger, or submission.

Crows and ravens can live for 20 years or more, but their average lifespan in the wild is from 5 to 7 years. Predators kill crows, but like humans, crows can die from many causes, including malnutrition, cold, environmental poisons, physical injury, birth defects, and a wide range of diseases. One of the toughest diseases they face is West Nile virus. It is spread by mosquitoes and attacks at least 17 different species of birds. It seems to hit crows especially hard. It can also infect humans.

Distribution

If you visit Europe, Asia, India, or Africa, you will recognize black, sturdy-billed birds as part of the crow family. Crows live everywhere on the planet except Antarctica, South America, and New Zealand.

The world's first crow-like birds lived in Australia. This small population increased in number and expanded its range. As they moved to new habitats over time, isolated groups formed new species.

Today, there are more than 45 species that belong to the genus *Corvus*, and many can be immediately recognized as crows. The northern raven, *Corvus corax*—the largest crow in North America—is the most common crow in the world.

Ravens

In addition to being the largest member of the crow family, with a wingspan of 4 feet (1.2 m), ravens differ from other members of the crow family in several ways. For one, they are more afraid of humans—and with good cause. Their populations have been erased throughout large regions of the world since they are believed to destroy more crops and farm animals than their smaller crow cousins do.

Crows and ravens live in many different kinds of habitats,
from deserts to mountains to tundras.

In North America, ravens have moved to regions where few humans live. They now live in a wide range of habitats—deserts, mountains, rocky coastlines, tundra, and alpine environments. There is an established population in the Appalachian Mountains, which shows that ravens may be expanding their range.

Chapter 2

Family Life

Organization

CROWS AND RAVENS live in family groups of about five to nine members. The group consists of one mating pair and several other members, called auxiliaries. These auxiliaries include offspring from the mated pair—mostly two- and three-year-olds—and occasionally birds that are four to five years old. The number of auxiliaries is determined by living conditions: food supply, availability of nesting sites, numbers of predators, and competition with other crows for territory.

At the age of two or three, young crows usually leave their families in the autumn and join temporary flocks, where they may look for a mate. Although all crows look alike to us, family members can easily recognize one another, even at long distances. Experts are not sure exactly how they do this.

In the spring, crows that are three years old or older usually find mates. Males tend to mate at an older

Mated crows and ravens stay together for life.

age than females. A mating pair stays together for life, and they lead their family group, making decisions such as where to build the nest and where to look for food. Crows are very loyal to their families and will risk their lives to protect family members.

Courtship Rituals

Courtship begins in the spring. New bonds are strengthened with mutual **preening**, sleeping side by side, giving gifts, rubbing beaks, and making soft sounds. The gifts given during courtship are often food brought by the male to the female to show that he will be a good provider. When the male brings food, the female may crouch low, with her feathers ruffled and mouth opened wide—like a baby bird, or **fledgling**. Gifts may also include bright objects such as a piece of tinfoil or shiny metal.

Male crows often perform daring and graceful acrobatic feats to impress the females. The males soar and tumble and turn loops in the air. If two males are both trying to impress the same female, they will bow to one another, moving their heads up and down, before they begin to compete.

Nest Building

A newly mated pair of crows settles in a territory that the male defends. The female chooses the nesting site and puts the nest together. The nesting site may

When crows are courting, the male will often give the female gifts, including food and bright, shiny objects that the male finds on the ground.

be high in an evergreen tree, but other trees will do. Other popular nesting sites include cliffs, building ledges, and church steeples—any place that is high and difficult for predators to get to.

While the female is building the nest, her mate feeds her. The male also brings her sticks and other building materials for the nest. In later years, the mated pair's grown offspring will help build the nest. It may take up to two weeks to complete the nest.

The ideal site for a crow's nest is in a grove of tall pine or spruce trees located near a pond or stream. The nest is sometimes built 60 feet (18m) or more above the ground to keep predators (including humans) away.

The female crow weaves sticks together to form a base about 2 to 3 feet (0.6 to 0.9 m) in diameter. After the base is finished, she uses finer material, such as strips of bark and smaller branches, to weave a bowl-like structure about 6 inches (15 cm) deep. The inner lining is made of grass, moss, feathers, or hair—anything soft. Mud and moss are used to hold everything together. After the nest is finished, the female may rest for a week or two. This may be a way to build up her strength to lay eggs and **incubate** them.

Mating

As the nest nears completion, the female crow is ready for young and she becomes receptive to mating. Courting crow couples perch close together and make different sounds, including low gurgling, coos, and a host of other low, strange sounds.

Crows may mate for a period of up to three weeks. After they mate, the male and female often spend time together in or near the nest. They may show their togetherness by touching bills or cleaning each other's feathers. The male may also bring the female food. These special couple behaviors, however, may not always been seen. Crows mate for life, so older pairs do not usually perform the same acts as younger, newer couples.

As they build their nests, female crows take leaves, feathers, and other soft materials to form an inner lining.

Family Bonds and the Role of Helpers

One of the most fascinating aspects of crow and raven life is the strength of family bonds. Most species of birds raise their young until they can survive independently, then the bonds between parent and offspring break. The young fend for themselves and the parents no longer recognize their offspring. This is not the case with crows. The **nestlings** born in the spring remain with their parents through the winter and help raise next year's offspring.

STUDY OF NORTHWESTERN CROW FAMILIES

Northwestern crows, whose scientific name is *Corvus courinus*, live on the coastal islands and shoreline of western Canada, southern Alaska, and the Aleutian Islands. A study revealed that the one-year-old crow's most vital function is to help protect the young. The one-year-olds were very active in protecting the food supply by keeping other crows and predators from trespassing. The one-year-olds helped feed the young, but their contributions were minor and the parents were the main source of food. Surprisingly, helpers begged for and received food that was meant for the chicks from the male parent. This was taken to be an incentive to protect the nest.

In comparing the success of nesting parents with helpers to those without, the ones with helpers were more successful. Evidently, the added protection of helpers was worth the cost.

The bonds of family are so strong that crows will visit their parents from time to time. Crows have a strong drive to be part of a family, and a lone crow will go to great lengths to be accepted by one.

While living with their parents, yearlings and older offspring help with nest building, feeding and caring for the nestlings, finding food for the family, defending the territory against neighboring crows, and protecting the nest and the family from predators. Once in a while, too many helpers get involved in nest building and are temporarily driven away by the mated pair.

While the female sits on the eggs, her mate and the auxiliary helpers of the family bring her food.

Eggs—A Family Project

A newly mated pair that is raising its first family has no auxiliary crows to help. In later years, raising a family will be much easier, since there will be other family members to help.

The female usually lays four to eight eggs that are bluish-green with brown splotches. She sits on the nest and incubates the eggs for 18 days. During this time, she is fed three to four times each hour. She has a distinct call she uses to ask for food, and her mate tears up the food before giving it to her.

After a while, she leaves the nest for a few minutes now and then to stretch her wings, move around, and even take a short flight. During incubation, the male works hard to stand guard to fight off any predators or neighboring crows.

Chapter **3**

Growing Up

The Nestlings Hatch

WHEN CROW AND RAVEN NESTLINGS hatch, there is a lot of excitement. The dominant male and the auxiliaries visit the nest just to see the new arrivals. The nestlings are born naked and blind. They are thin-skinned with bluish bumps where their feathers will eventually be and have a huge bulging belly. Their large naked head is so heavy that it wobbles when lifted. Almost immediately after they hatch, nestlings start crying for food, and they eat constantly. The gaping mouths of the chicks have a bright pink lining that triggers the adults' instinct to feed the young.

The male and the auxiliaries feed both the female and the nestlings. The male will also spend time standing guard over the nest.

Raising the Young

The largest pieces of food are torn up in bits and mixed with saliva before being fed to the nestlings. The saliva serves as a source of water and perhaps other substances, such as digestive **enzymes**.

The nestlings excrete waste, or feces, in sacs made of membranes that the adults then take away. As the chicks get stronger, they lift their rear ends high so their fecal sacs can be removed and flipped over the side of the nest. Later, they learn to defecate, or dispose of feces, right over the edge of the nest.

FAMILY PLANNING

In a natural process called **imprinting**, newly hatched goslings will follow the first living object they see after hatching. With many birds, this period of imprinting is fairly short. For crows and ravens, imprinting takes several weeks. If a crow is imprinted by a human being at an early age, the human and his or her family become the crow's family. The crow will give these people all of the loyalty it would give to its own family in the wild.

The Life of Fledglings

The nestlings' eyes open after 5 days, and their feathers begin to appear after 10 days. The chicks have all their feathers at 28 days, and they are ready to leave the nest about 30 to 35 days after hatching. Individual fledglings may stand on the side of the nest or on a nearby branch to stretch and exercise their wings.

The first flight is usually clumsy, but they learn quickly and are making short flights in the trees within a short time. The young crows continue to be fed by adults during the next 10 days or so as they learn to feed themselves by watching family members. Eventually, they take on adult status in the group. The following year, they may replace or join their older siblings in helping to rear the young.

Tragedy at a Nest

A hungry raccoon, possum, or weasel may climb a tree and eat young crows in a nest. At such times, all of the crows in a family will work together to try to distract and fight off the intruder. Sometimes they succeed. But usually, when the attacker is a large animal, the nest is lost.

Hail, heavy rainstorms, and strong winds can also destroy crow nests, leaving the young to die on the ground. Often, the crows will have time to build another nest and raise another **brood** in the same season.

Family Care

After the fledglings mature, the family group stays together and roosts in a favorite place, such as a dense grove of trees within its territory. At sunrise, the family members leave the roost to bathe and preen. Bathing may be done in a stream, pond, or puddle of water in which the crows can splash and ruffle their feathers. In winter, they may flutter around in soft snow to get clean.

Mutual grooming involves one crow preening another, especially around the head, eyes, and neck—areas where it is difficult for crows to clean themselves. Preening cleans parasites and loose feathers from the skin and repairs damaged feathers. Crows with disabilities, such as a crossed bill that makes it hard to preen themselves, are preened by others in the family. Mutual grooming reinforces bonds within the family.

To rid themselves of parasites, crows will sometimes lie on an anthill and allow the ants to crawl over them. The ants remove lice and other pests from the crows' bodies. Apparently, ant bites do not hurt the crows.

Chapter 4

Finding
Food

The Search for Food

AFTER BATHING AND PREENING, the search for food begins. A group of crows or ravens takes off together toward a feeding area, usually one that has been chosen by the dominant male. The first stop may be a fast-food restaurant dumpster, a supermarket parking lot, or a favorite cornfield. The crows spread out on the site and make a thorough search. When they finish with one site, they head for another. In the afternoon, they often stop in some favorite place to rest or take a nap.

Crows and ravens take food wherever they can find it, including from dumpsters, parking lots, or fields.

Remember that both crows and ravens are scavengers. They can eat meat, vegetables, fruit, dead mice, and whatever else they find. They have learned to tear up plastic garbage bags, releasing and spreading out whatever is inside. They also clean up dropped french fries and bits of hamburgers from fast-food parking lots.

Body language, such as a curious turn of the head, can let others know about a newfound source of food. Various calls throughout the day also maintain contact between different individuals and the entire group. Experts have identified about 25 different calls.

Each crow has a unique call that may involve some odd sounds, such as a sharp bark or screech. This makes it easy for the group to keep track of the whereabouts of each individual. Other crows in the family may imitate an individual's call to make contact. Calls that identify individuals are not like names, however. They often change over time.

What They Eat

Crows are omnivorous and eat almost anything: berries, grubs, grasshoppers, carrion (dead animals), snails, frogs, bird eggs, nuts, clams, fish, tender plant seedlings, mice, and worms. One study of the stomach contents of crows revealed 650 kinds of food. Crows and ravens have a curiosity and willingness to taste almost any food. This is a real advantage in helping them survive, as is their habit of sometimes having one member of the family serve as a guard while the others eat. Individual crows will store food in a variety of places—under the bark of trees, under bushes or tufts of grass, under the shingles of a roof, in a pile of rocks. This is a way to save food for use during hard times or while preparing for a new family. Crows have excellent memories, and they seldom forget about a stash of food. In fact, crows visit their hiding places often to check on their food.

Crows, like owls, will throw up pellets of undigested matter, such as bone, fur, and feathers. You can often find these pellets under their nests.

Eating Road Kill

Dead cattle, dead soldiers on a battlefield, or dead animals in the road are easy meals for crows. Crows are unable to penetrate tough hides, so they have to depend on larger predators or scavengers to get the carcasses open. They approach a new carcass with extreme caution, and often jump straight up several times before pecking at the body. Even with this caution, some people claim that, unlike vultures, crows do not always wait for death before they start to feed.

Crows have learned to judge how fast cars are going, no matter which direction they are going. This helps the crows get a few extra pecks at a piece of road kill before they have to fly away for safety.

Unusual Ways to Get Food

Crows in the southern United States have been seen hanging upside down and shaking branches to release insects, spiders, and small lizards to crows waiting below. This is learned behavior. The young crows watch adults, share the food, and eventually take a turn shaking the trees. Cooperation among crows is one more advantage of living together in groups.

Some crows have been seen getting food in some unusual ways. Some crows will shake branches to knock insects and other prey out, so the crows waiting below can eat.

Crows in a field of sweet corn are a real problem because they go from cob to cob stripping the husks and eating a few kernels from each cob. Damaged cobs can't be sold. (Corn grown for cattle feed is not affected because cows will still eat the damaged cobs.) Crows also love young corn shoots. Before insecticides were used, people were willing to tolerate the damage crows did to cornfields because crows also ate insects, which were an even bigger problem. Today, the population of crows has been greatly reduced in corn country. Corporate farms have destroyed many of the wooded boundaries and thick hedgerows that separated smaller family farms and served as nesting and roosting sites for crows.

Enjoying Hard-to-Eat Foods

Crows learn by observing. They may have learned how to open clams by watching flying seagulls drop them onto hard pavement. Crows open clams the same way and have extended the technique, dropping nuts on roads to crack them open.

In Port Townsend, Washington, people have reported seeing crows drop chestnuts in busy street intersections. Locals concluded that the crows know there is a good chance that the chestnuts will be crushed by passing cars.

Crows seem to like to dunk their food in water before eating it. The reason for this is not clear.

Ravens and crows learn how to open hard-to-eat foods, such as nuts, by watching other animals do it. Once they have opened the tough shells, they often take the food back to a safe place to eat it.

Wetting the food might soften it and make it easier to swallow, or somehow make the food more enjoyable. Crows also just seem to enjoy dropping things into water. They sometimes pick up golf balls and drop them into ponds. The reason? They may think they have found a nut or it may just be their way of having fun.

Learning About New Foods

Crows cooperate with each other. When one crow finds a new source of food, such as a nest of mice, it will call others over. The other crows gather around and study the new find. Usually, when the original discoverer of the food is done eating, the most dominant crow will eat, and then the next dominant after that, until all of the birds have eaten. Crows will not try to steal food from a family member. This behavior is very important in learning about new food sources and in keeping the family group together. The combination of curiosity, diversity in food gathering, and cooperation and loyalty within the family shows a complex social structure with strong survival value.

Chapter 5

Crow Behavior

Are Crows Intelligent?

DO OTHER SPECIES THINK? Do they use reason in every-day life? For many years, two criteria have been used to establish the uniqueness of human intelligence: tool making and solving complex problems.

Tool Making

Crows in New Caledonia (located between Australia and Fiji) regularly make and use a modified stem as a tool to remove insects from **detritus** that collects in the crevices and holes of woody plants. These tools are remarkable.

They are uniform in design, involve careful work, and have hooks. (The invention of hooks by early humans is considered a major advance in technology.)

Once the tool is made, the crow will use its beak or foot to carry it from place to place. When eating, the crow places the tool to one side or holds it with one foot. The crow will even return to pick up the tool if it is left behind. Other crows watch and learn how to make and use tools.

Problem Solving

In one test of intelligence for crows and ravens, University of Vermont biologist Bernd Heinrich dangled food on the ends of strings. This presented a problem that the crows had never seen before. They had to figure out how to get the food. Crows couldn't solve the problem, but three out of five ravens did. Within seconds, they pulled up loops of the string and then held them with their feet. Many people believe ravens are the most intelligent birds. If so, crows are a close second.

Other Signs of Crow Intelligence

Crows will ignore a person who is carrying a broom or rake over his shoulder, but they will flee from a person carrying a shotgun. They can not only tell the difference, but they also know from experience that guns kill crows.

Scientists learned about the superior intelligence of ravens by designing problems for them to solve. One test involved getting food that was dangling from a string. Although crows couldn't figure out how to get the food, ravens understood that they could use loops in the string to pull up the food and eat it.

People have observed that when three hunters enter a **blind** under the watchful eyes of crows, and two of the hunters leave, the crows know that one person is still inside. However, if five hunters enter the blind and four leave, the crows will think that all the people have left. This indicates that crows can count to three. To crows, there are four numbers: 1, 2, 3, and "many."

Crows are exceptionally intelligent, compared both with other birds and with mammals. The evolution of intelligence is thought to be linked to social structure. Crows pass on the knowledge they gain through experience to others because of the strong bonding in their social groups. The relationship of the mated male and female, the family helpers, and families that roost together all offer opportunities for learning from one another.

Defending Territory

The territory of a crow family unit is vital to the family's survival since it ensures their food supply and nesting sites. It must be vigorously defended.

If another flock of crows flies over the territory and is obviously on its way someplace else, the home crows will do nothing. But if the intruders come by in search of food, the crows immediately defend their area. The result is a midair encounter that involves loud cries, "dive bombing," and even some pecking, until the intruders are driven off.

A more serious incident occurs when intruders land in another group's territory and begin to eat. In one recorded encounter, a neighboring flock crossed a fence that defined the territory of its neighbor and proceeded to search for food. The crows that claimed the territory spotted the intruders and sounded an "assembly call." The defending crows responded by gathering in trees that overlooked the field. After some cawing, the dominant male of the defending group flew in and landed in the middle of the intruders. Alone, he made loud caws and began to attack

When ravens or crows feel threatened, they sound an assembly call to get the attention of other crows. This tells the others to prepare to fight off the threat.

individual intruders. Shortly after the lone attack by the dominant male, all the defending crows flew in together to attack the intruders. The intruding crows quickly left the area, and were pursued by the defenders.

The human observer who saw this event drew several conclusions. The entire response by the defending crows was planned and coordinated. The dominant male led the attack while the others held back until the time was right to act. It is likely that some kind of command was given to tell the others to attack because they all moved at once. The encounter did not result in any serious injury to either the intruders or the defenders.

Mobbing the Enemy

It is well known that a stuffed owl can be used to draw crows. When a crow sees an owl, an assembly call is sounded and crows begin to gather. The crows attack with a vengeance, cawing loudly and even pecking at the owl. The noise will sometimes attract neighboring crows, making the attack even more raucous. This is one time when trespassing is tolerated. When there is no longer a threat, the crows go their separate ways.

More frequently, crows and ravens attack a hawk. If the hawk flies away, the crows take off after it, attacking from different directions. Sometimes they actually make contact. The goal is to make the hawk so uncomfortable that it cannot hunt. If the hawk lands in a tree, the crows will land close by or even in the same tree. When the hawk takes off again, the crows fly right behind it. Sometimes, the noise the crows make attracts other crows from nearby flocks and even other bird species, and they all join in to harass the hawk. Crows have been known to drive hawks to the ground. Eventually, the hawk realizes that it won't be able to hunt and leaves the crows' territory. If you are lucky enough to witness such an encounter, you may see the hawk or owl turn rapidly in midair to ward off a crow. There are several accounts of hawks grabbing a crow in midair and killing it.

Mobbing works both ways. Small birds will mob crows that threaten their young. Even a single sparrow has been known to drive off a crow.

Roosting Together

Crows and ravens crave the company of other birds of their kind. Auxiliaries will sometimes take a short break from family chores to roost with other crows. When nesting is over and the need to defend their territory decreases, different crow families will often roost together.

In the fall, crows expand their search for food. With cold weather, many crows, especially those that live in Canada, migrate south. Crows that live in regions with mild winters may stay where they are.

In the fall and winter, different flocks of crows from different regions tend to roost together in favored locations, such as a grove of trees sheltered from the wind. In Springfield, Ohio, for example, as many as 150,000 roosting crows have been spotted. In Chatham, Ontario, 160,000 crows roost in trees above homes. These winter roosts may last four to five months. As crows fly in from all directions, the chatter is loud and continuous as disputes arise over roosting sites. At night, the noise quiets down a bit,

Large flocks of crows—as many as hundreds of thousands of individual birds—are often seen roosting together.

although there are many strange grunts, coos, growls, and whispers that have unknown meanings.

Night is the most dangerous time for crows. It is then that their most dreaded enemy, owls—especially the great horned owl—have a distinct advantage. An owl can swoop in on silent wings and take away a sleeping crow. Studies at the University of Indiana have shown that birds under pressure from predators literally sleep with one eye open and half of their brain awake. This way, they can snooze and still be able to tell when a predator is approaching.

In the morning, hungry crows may follow well-fed crows to their sources of food. Some groups travel 30 miles (48 km) or more. A newly discovered food source is often shared with other crows. Sharing sometimes establishes lasting friendships between unattached crows that later lead to mating, and a lone crow may be accepted by a group.

Large flocks are good for survival. Sleeping close together offers the safety of numbers. Experts wonder, though, why crows form groups of thousands. A predator would have just as hard a time sneaking up on 20 crows as it would on 10,000 crows. Probably the most logical explanation for the large numbers of roosting crows is the strong drive among the birds to be part of a group. Crows simply enjoy the company of other crows, just as people often like to spend time together.

The night is the most dangerous time for crows. During the dark hours of the night, crows are vulnerable to attacks from many predators.

Crows at Play

Some writers insist that play, like thinking, is exclusively a human trait, but they are wrong. Crows do play, and if you ever see them play, you will know it instantly. Not only do they play, but they seem to have a real sense of humor.

To steal a fish from an otter, one crow will distract the otter by pulling at its tail while another crow steals the fish. Crows use the same trick on eagles. The eagles usually end up losing a few tail feathers. Crows have been seen pestering other animals for no apparent reason except for the fun of it. However, when a

EYEWITNESS ACCOUNT OF CROW FAMILY BEHAVIOR

Homeowner Alice Hayes reported this event that she observed from her window overlooking Lake Michigan: A crow was desperately struggling to stay afloat in the water while another flew overhead, swooping down low and noisily cawing encouragement. After about 10 minutes of flapping its wings trying to stay afloat, the drowning crow got tired and sank beneath the surface.

Alice left the window, but returned a little while later to see six crows on a rail bordering the lake. All of the crows were facing the lake and looking at the place where their family member had disappeared. Evidently, the one crow that witnessed the drowning had communicated with other family members and led them to the site of the tragedy.

crow plays with another animal, it learns something about that animal. Knowing the other species that live in its environment helps crows survive.

A favorite game is to hang by one foot from a telephone wire, and crows have been seen passing a piece of food back and forth from beak to foot while hanging upside down. Crows also will drop a stick and see if they can catch it before it hits the ground. Another favorite game is tug-of-war with a stick.

Crows are often seen watching and playing with other animals. Scientists believe they do this to learn more about the other animal's behavior.

When one crow starts a game, others will often join in, repeating the actions of the first crow.

Crows have been seen sliding down a snowbank on their backs, then climbing up the bank and sliding down again. This play resembles what river otters do. Crows have also been known to plunge into soft snowbanks. These habits may have developed from the way crows clean themselves in snow when no water is available.

Crows will play with a variety of objects. One crow was seen lying on its back and tossing a crumpled piece of paper into the air with its beak and feet. Agility is a trait crows need to survive. Play of this type may help develop agility.

Crows will swing back and forth on strands of Spanish moss, with their beaks pointed downward. Spanish moss is often pulled off trees and used as nesting material in the southern United States. This game might have sprung from that activity.

Chapter 6

Crows and People

Pet Crows and Ravens

CROWS AND RAVENS ARE considered **migratory** birds, and so ownership of crows is a federal offense. The law is a good one because it prevents the capture and sale of crows, but it also has its drawbacks.

What should you do if you find a baby crow? If it can fly even only a short distance or tries to fly away from you, it's best to leave it alone. Its family will care for it. If it's not fully feathered (which means it is less than

Although ravens and crows are intelligent, beautiful birds, they do not make good pets. In fact, it is against the law to keep a crow as a pet.

four weeks old), however, it will probably die if left alone. That is a problem.

A bird that is only three to four weeks old is not yet imprinted and will accept food readily. An older bird can be helped, but will never be tamed. If you take a crow home, place it in a shoebox with soft paper or rags. Don't place crows in birdcages. You might be able to bring the crow to a licensed wildlife rehabilitator, who will take in young or injured birds free of charge. You might seek help from a vet or refer to the Internet for advice on diet and care. An injured crow should be helped with the intention of releasing it, not keeping it as a permanent pet. Baby birds raised properly can be released in the fall, so they will be able to join newly forming flocks of young crows.

Everyday Life With a Crow

Aside from being intelligent and interesting, crows have the added attraction of mimicking sounds. Crows are not as vocal as parrots, but their ability to mimic sounds makes them very interesting animals. The next time you see a crow, give two short, rapid caws, and then repeat this double caw. The double caw is a territorial call and is likely to be repeated. The crow may even imitate the way you make the caw sound. Crows have been known to imitate the meow of a cat, the bark of a dog, or the cluck of a chicken.

Ravens and crows can sometimes imitate sounds that people make.

A crow has been seen teasing a sleeping dog. As soon as the dog dozed off, the crow would sneak up and pull its tail, and then quickly fly off. The dog would wake up, startled, and then look around and go back to sleep. The crow repeated the behavior until the bewildered dog finally left.

Considering all the different types of interaction crows and ravens have with humans, some people believe that the crow truly understands human nature. Most crows have learned to live intimately with humans and to take advantage of every opportunity that comes along, while always remaining just a little bit suspicious.

blind—An enclosure from which hunters shoot birds or other game.

brood—A group of offspring all born in the same season.

detritus—Loose material that results from disintegration.

DNA—Deoxyribonucleic acid; nucleic acids that make up the genes that are responsible for passing traits from one parents to their offspring.

enzymes—Proteins that help speed up chemical reactions, such as the breakdown of food in the stomach.

fledgling—A young bird that has just developed the feathers it needs to fly.

imprinting—A process by which a newborn or very young animal learns to recognize and be attracted to a parent or something or someone acting as a parent.

incubate—Sit on eggs to help them hatch with the warmth of the mother's body.

iridescent—Appearing multicolored in bright light.

migratory—Moving from one area to another with the change of the seasons.

nestlings—A young bird that cannot yet fly and still lives in the nest.

nictitating—Refers to the thin membrane, found in many animals with backbones, beneath the lower lid of the eye that can extend across the whole eyeball.

omnivorous—Feeding on both animals and plants.

preening—Grooming the feathers.

scavenger—An animal that feeds on dead animals.

American Society for Crows and Ravens. Available online at *http://www.ascaronline.org*.

McGowan, Kevin J. "Family Lives of the Uncommon American Crow." *Cornell Plantations Magazine* 51 (1) (1996).

Feher-Elston, Catherine. *Ravensong*. Flagstaff, AZ: Northland Publishing, 1991.

Heinrich, Bernd. *Mind of the Raven*. New York: Harper Collins, 1999.

Hunt, Gavin R. "Manufacture and Use of Hook-Tools by New Caledonian Crows." *Nature* 379 (1996): 249–251.

Kilham, Lawrence. *The American Crow and Common Raven*. College Station, TX: Texas A&M University Press, 1989.

———. "Play-Like Behaviour of American Crows." *Florida Field Naturalist* 12 (2): (1984): 33–36.

Madge, Steve, and Hilary Burn. *Crows and Jays, A Guide to the Crows, Jays and Magpies of the World*. Boston: Houghton Mifflin Company, 1994.

Pringle, Lawrence. *Listening to the Crows*. New York: Cromwell Co., 1976.

Savage, Candace. *Bird Brains*. San Francisco: Sierra Club, 1995.

Verbeek, N., and R. Butler. "Cooperative Breeding of the American Crow." *Journal of Field Ornithology* 55 (1984): 349–356.

———. "Cooperative Breeding of the Northwestern Crow, *C. courinus* in British Columbia." *The Ibis* 123 (1981): 183–189.

Feher-Elston, Catharine. *Ravensong: A Natural And Fabulous History Of Ravens And Crows*. Tarcher, 2005.

Marzluff, John M., and Tony Angell. *In the Company of Crows and Ravens*. New Haven, CT: Yale University Press, 2005.

Savage, Candace. *Crows: Encounters with the Wise Guys*. Vancouver: Greystone Books, 2005.

Web Sites

American Society for Crows and Ravens. Available online at *http://www.ascaronline.org*.

"Keep the American Crow Alive and Well." Save the Crows. Available online at *http://www.savethecrows.org/*.

"The Language and Culture of Crows." Crows.net. Available online at *http://www.crows.net/*.

PICTURE CREDITS

page:

8: © Kris Mercer/Shutterstock.com
9: © Marcy J. Levinson/
  Shutterstock.com
12: © Ilya D. Gridnev/
  Shutterstock.com
13: © Vladimir Ivanov/
  Shutterstock.com
14: © Sherrianne Talon/
  Shutterstock.com
17: © Kaleb Timberlake/
  Shutterstock.com
20: © Renata Fedosova/
  Shutterstock.com
22: © William Bradley
24: © Peter von Bucher/
  Shutterstock.com

26: © William Bradley
33: © Vitaliy Berkovych/
  Shutterstock.com
36: © William Bradley
38: © John Kirinic/Shutterstock.com
42: © William Bradley
44: © Yuriy Maksymenko/
  Shutterstock.com
47: © Samuel Acosta/Shutterstock.com
49: © EML/Shutterstock.com
51: © Ron Hilton/Shutterstock.com
54: © Matt Ragen/Shutterstock.com
56: © Hazeelin Hassan/
  Shutterstock.com

Cover: © Matt Ragen/Shutterstock.com

ABOUT THE AUTHOR

James V. Bradley taught biology at Lake Forest High School in Lake Forest, Illinois, for 25 years. He also taught science in Colorado and in the United Kingdom. Bradley received the Illinois STAR Award (Science Teaching Achievement Recognition) in 1980 and was named by the National Association of Biology Teachers as outstanding biology teacher in Illinois in 1981. He retired from teaching in 1994, but continues to write and study science topics.